Made in United States
Troutdale, OR
10/02/2024

23257867R00061